Essential Question
How does the Earth change?

Earthquakes

by Elizabeth Doering

What Is an Earthquake?

This shows an earthquake in San Francisco.

Picture this. Your house starts to shake. Dishes **rattle**. It could be an earthquake!

A large earthquake hit China in 2010.

Earthquakes happen all the time.
Some are big. Some are little.
Big earthquakes are big **news**.

There was an earthquake in Virginia in 2011. Millions of people felt it.

New York City

Washington, D.C.

Virginia

Understanding the Map
The star is the quake's center. The circles show where people felt the quake. People close to the star felt it most.

Japan has many earthquakes.

In 2011, a big earthquake hit Japan. It moved the ground 8 feet.

fault

fault

This is a fault.

Earthquakes often happen along fault lines. Fault lines are deep cracks in the ground.

Robert E. Wallace/U.S. Geological Survey

The Mississipi River was once hit by big earthquakes.

Big earthquakes hit the Mississippi River. They **caused** huge waves.

STOP AND CHECK

What have you learned about earthquakes so far?

What Causes Earthquakes?

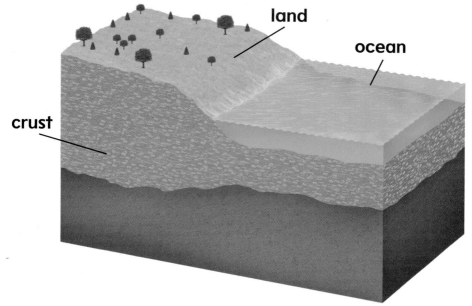

land

ocean

crust

The Earth's crust is under
the land and oceans.

What causes earthquakes?
The **surface** of **Earth** is called
the crust. The crust is not **solid**.
It is made of giant pieces.
The pieces are called plates.

Illustration: Rob Schuster

Earth's Plates

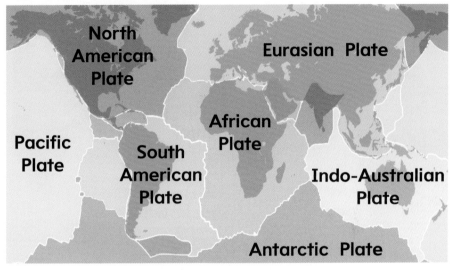

North American Plate

Eurasian Plate

African Plate

Pacific Plate

South American Plate

Indo-Australian Plate

Antarctic Plate

This map shows the plates that make up Earth's crust.

Plates

Earth's plates move. We don't feel it. They slide slowly. They push and pull. They can make rock deep in the Earth **explode**. This causes shock **waves**.

STOP AND CHECK

What causes shock waves?

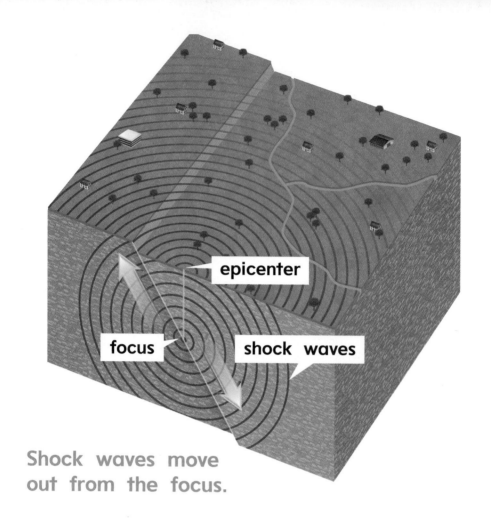

Shock waves move
out from the focus.

Shock Waves

Shock waves start underground.
The waves start at the focus.
They move through the ground.
Some shock waves **reach** the
surface. This causes earthquakes.

Giant waves can cause lots of damage.

A quake's epicenter is above the focus. The quake is strongest here.

Earthquakes happen underwater, too. This can cause giant waves.

STOP AND CHECK

Where do earthquakes begin?

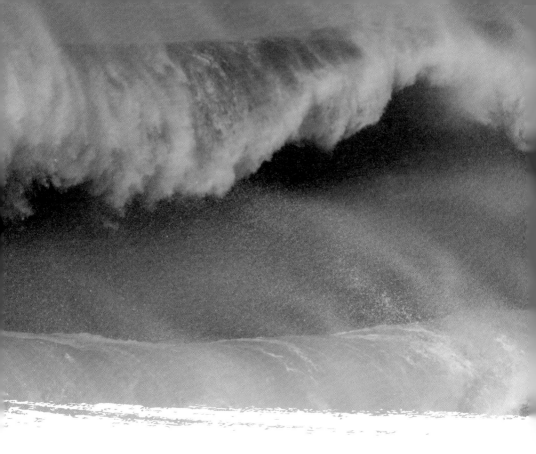

Tsunami

Tsunami are giant ocean waves. They can be as tall as buildings when they hit the **shore**. They are powerful. They can be dangerous!

This is what a tsunami looks like.

Tsunami waves start small.
Near land they suck up water.
This makes them grow taller
and wider. A tsunami looks like
a giant wall of water.

STOP AND CHECK

What are some effects
of earthquakes?

How Strong Are Earthquakes?

This machine tells how strong an earthquake is.

Some earthquakes are big. Most are small. There will always be earthquakes. But now we know much more about them.

Rick Wilking/Reuters/Corbis

Long ago in China, people used this. Water came out when the earth shook. It went into a frog's mouths.

This can make it safer for people.

STOP AND CHECK

Are most earthquakes big or small?

Science & Society Picture Library/Getty Images

Respond to Reading

Summarize

Summarize *Earthquakes.* Use the chart to help you.

Cause → Effect

Text Evidence

1. What can underwater earthquakes cause?

   Cause and Effect

2. Read the word *focus* on page 10. Use the words and diagram. How can you tell what *focus* means? Vocabulary

3. Write about why earthquakes happen. Write About Reading

Read Together

Compare Texts
Read to find out how glaciers change Earth.

Glaciers

Glaciers are made of ice, snow, rock, and water. They form on cold mountain tops. The snow piles up. New snow crushes the snow below. The snow below becomes ice. The ice slides down. Slowly, a glacier starts.

Some glaciers look blue.

Rivers of Ice

Glaciers move. They flow like rivers. The moving ice and rock can change the land.

This is a glacier.
A piece is falling into the ocean.

There are glaciers around the world. Most glaciers are high in the mountains. It is cooler there.

Melting Glaciers

Glaciers can melt. Most of the Earth's fresh water is inside glaciers. What if all that ice melted?

Make Connections
How do earthquakes change Earth?
Essential Question

How are glaciers like tsunami?
Text to Text

Focus on
Science

Purpose To make a model of an earthquake

What to Do

Step 1 Work outside with a group. Bring a baking pan, two pieces of fabric, some soil, and an eraser.

Step 2 Place the fabric in the pan. Let the sides hang out. Press soil into the pan. Stand the eraser on the soil.

Step 3 Now, pull the sides of the fabric in opposite directions.

Conclusion Describe the results.